THE
SELF-REGULATION
WORKBOOK

FOR 3- TO 5-YEAR-OLDS

PLAY-BASED & CREATIVE ACTIVITIES TO BUILD COPING SKILLS AND HANDLE BIG EMOTIONS

ABBRÉ MCCLAIN, PSY.D, LCPC
JACQUELINE SALAZAR, PSY.D, LCPC

ULYSSES PRESS

Published by:
Ulysses Books for Young Readers,
an imprint of Ulysses Press
PO Box 3440
Berkeley, CA 94703
www.ulyssespress.com

ISBN: 978-1-64604-7-291

Printed in the United States
10 9 8 7 6 5 4 3 2 1

Acquisitions editor: Claire Sielaff
Managing editor: Claire Chun
Editor: Renee Rutledge
Proofreader: Sherian Brown
Front cover design: Akangksha Sarmah
Cover artwork: children © FoxyImage/shutterstock.com; shapes and objects © aliasching
   /shutterstock.com
Interior design and production: what!design @ whatweb.com
Interior art: © Davidenco/shutterstock.com except master page icons © aliasching
   /shutterstock.com; mirror on page 32 © fire_fly/shutterstock.com; pets on page 39
   © Katflare/shutterstock.com; icons on page 74 © mi-vector/shutterstock.com

This book is dedicated to the little ones in our personal and professional lives.
Thank you for allowing us to sit in the seat of humility.
We do what we do because of you.

CONTENTS

iNTRoDuCTioN

This book is written specifically for the people in what we like to call the "village"—all the adults in a young human's life who care about them and are invested in their well-being. This includes (and is not limited to) parents, caregivers, extended family, daycare providers, teachers, and therapists who work with young children and families.

As therapists who believe in and work within the context of culture and community, we understand the importance of the ecological well-being of young children, particularly those ages three to five. There are so many ways that children spend time in their environment and begin building attachments, connections, and relationships with others. This fosters a sense of safety and trust across home, school, and their neighborhood community.

With this in mind, we hope this workbook gives you access to resources that facilitate your continuing to provide safe and affirming spaces for young children. This book is designed to help children as well as the caring adults in their lives to thrive in their strengths and personal best. We hope you find inspiration in these pages!

A NoTE To CAREGiVERS AND FAMiLiES

You are one of the most important people to children and are a key figure in their physical, psychological, and emotional world. Whenever they leave home, they take you with them both in their mind and heart, and they may take something from home as well (like a toy or blanket) just to remind them of that special place you share. You are their very first understanding of this big world, and that is exactly where we want you to be!

We understand the beauty of diverse family constellations in which caring adults within the family network can be biological parents, adoptive parents, grandparents, godparents, aunts and uncles, cousins, nannies or babysitters, and close friends in your community. Children can never have too big of a support system to provide guidance throughout their lives.

This book can be of great service to you and your children, as it can guide you through intentional ways of being together, building trust, creating safety, and supporting your children's feelings.

A NOTE TO TEACHERS, DAYCARE PROVIDERS, AND EDUCATIONAL LEADERSHIP

You are essential to the fabric of development and wellness with children. Upon entry to school or early learning, children can spend equal to or even more time with you than any other caring adults in their day! Both the quantity and quality of this time is so important, and young children are often ready and waiting to be affirmed and included in this new space of learning. Under your care and guidance, children gain tools for exploration, curiosity, trust, industry, and motivation, which are essential for academic and social-emotional learning.

This book can be useful for both individual and classroom-wide activities to continue fostering a safe and nurturing relational space. We are immensely grateful to you for your role in helping to shape the growing minds of the future!

A NOTE TO THERAPISTS

You have the unique privilege of working with and for children, as well as interacting and advocating in the systems in which they spend most of their time (i.e., home, school, and community). Your knowledge of holistic child development, the importance of early learning, youth mental health, family wellness, community support, and optimal health being dependent upon the above-mentioned pillars is vital to the coordinated care you provide in advocacy of your very young clients. For you, this book may be useful in your own clinical practice with young children and families. This may particularly be the case for family-based sessions and parent-related intervention. You might also find this workbook useful in consultative practice with daycares, preschools, community centers, pediatric wellness centers, and any other place where young children spend their time. Your positioning within the work with families can be both dynamic and transformative, often being the initiating mechanism toward individual, family, and collective processes and supporting and guiding important playmakers in children's lives along the way. Thank you for the work that you do.

WHAT TO LOOK FORWARD TO THROUGHOUT THIS WORKBOOK

We hope that you feel a renewed sense of industry, curiosity, and excitement about yourself, the children you care about, and the relationship that you have together. In the next chapter, we we'll introduce essential science around just how important you are to your children or pupils. In the chapters that follow, we will share key information about attachment, developmental milestones, and the functions and benefits of play. In the final chapters, we will provide a space to apply the important tenets above through activities, reflective worksheets, and additional resources. Having you around in meaningful ways helps children to navigate their world in a way that supports their capacities to thrive at their personal best, no matter where they are. We hope this workbook shows you just how valuable you are to the children in your care!

CHAPTER 1

THE SCIENCE BEHIND
SELF-REGULATION

As coauthors and best friends, we could not be more different. We come from different backgrounds, yet we align in our firmly rooted shared values, especially our use of storytelling as it relates to connection. This is also the case with our careers, in which we care for youth and their families as supervisors, educators, and mental health practitioners. We even tell stories with cultural communication style differences that end up fitting together. For instance, Dr. McClain needs time and space to share the story, as she approaches storytelling through an immersive style, whereas Dr. Salazar needs little time and tells stories in a matter-of-fact style.

The children in your care may be drastically different from you, and that is okay! As a caregiver, teacher, or professional, you do not have to be just like them in order to provide care in the way that they need. Therefore, as the authors, we share our story to let you know that individual differences should be celebrated, and when one is able to have empathy and understand the lived experience of another, everyone can act in a way that contributes to regulation and attachment (the ability to build and maintain safe and secure relationships). These relationships serve as a template for how one sees themselves, others, and the world. The science behind attachment will be discussed further in this chapter. This use of storytelling, and how we all tell stories, serves to shape who we are and helps to maintain our connection as best friends. In the book *Big Friendship: How We Keep Each Other Close* (2020), authors Aminatou Sow and Ann Friedman discuss how friends also serve as attachment figures who provide connection and comfort. Therefore, through differences and similarities, we as authors and best friends serve as one another's attachment system and hold great significance in each other's lives.

The importance and power of relationships can never be overshared or underestimated. As humans, we cannot survive physically or emotionally without connection to other humans! This powerful and transformative process has a bidirectional and ecological impact on the people involved in the relationship, on the context or environment they are in, as well as on the relationship itself! This dynamic lives on throughout the lifespan of the relationship and can be replicated or reenacted, and permeate toward other relationships at home as well as in the community. For relationships to occur, there must have been a blueprint—an introduction and the first teachers around what relationships should look like. This is what science calls "attachment."

When children feel a sense of physical and emotional closeness, they can both see, feel, and believe that they are enveloped in care. The ability to be physically and emotionally safe also helps children to regulate during times of distress and have a launching or a rooted place (which is a person). Having this security gives them the permission to explore, grow, build developmental competencies, and manage emotional experiences in a healthy way. **Closeness, safety, and security** are three important positions that are the basis for which attachment, co-regulation, and self-regulation occur.

These three important positions are the basis for which co-regulation, individual emotional regulation, and self-regulation occur.

A SAFE AND SECURE BASE

The powerful relationship you have with your children, student, or client is the genesis for which all regulation can occur. Children's ability to regulate their own emotions is predicated on their ability to engage in co-regulation with you! In other words, it is essential that children can come to you with their feelings to learn about them so that they have a chance to apply that on their own and with their peers. To be this secure base for children, it is important that adults appraise our own regulatory capacities to be physically and emotionally available when the children need it the most.

A safe and secure relationship that children have with caring adults is the prerequisite for the mechanisms that help them begin to identify, understand, respond to, and regulate emotions. These gears do not begin to move simply because the relationship exists; instead, sustainable social-emotional development blossoms within the important meaning placed in the relationship by the child and safe adult. The regulatory space is where development in this area begins.

We are all born with the *capacity* to regulate our emotions. However, our *ability* to self-regulate needs to be built and shaped by a trusted adult starting as early as infancy with a particular importance of building such skill from birth through five years of age. It is important to mention that sometimes significant life events, stressors, diagnoses, and adverse childhood experiences, such as neglect and abuse, may impact young children's ability to master the skill of self-regulation during early development. However, while children facing obstacles and hardships early in life may need a bit more time, practice, and empathy to master the skill of self-regulation, they too can develop the ability to regulate their strong emotions. Therefore, this book is geared toward all children, including those with disabilities, mental health difficulties, behavioral problems, and those children who are simply creative and imaginative. However, to truly understand self-regulation capacities and abilities within young children, adults must first understand the building blocks of child development that contribute to being able to master this complex skill of self-regulation.

Take a moment to reflect on a significant person, especially when you were a young child. Who do you envision? What did you notice yourself feeling in the memory and as you reflected? How have they shaped the person you are today? As we reflect on our own formative years, many of us can recall at least one significant person that made a positive imprint on us, whether that was a caregiver, best friend, teacher, clinician/doctor, or other important community or religious figure. The main purpose of this book is to cultivate that role of an important figure by fostering a safe, secure, and playful relationship during young children's developmental years. This relationship becomes the vessel of building self-regulation in young children.

DEVELOPMENTAL MILESTONES

All children develop differently and uniquely, especially in the early years (ages zero to five) of development. Developmental milestones are skills and tasks that most children can do by a certain age. They help assess and provide clues about the trajectory of the children's development. Some children develop skills and master tasks earlier or later, which fall in the realm of normal development. However, if children are not meeting certain or several developmental milestones, this raises cause for concern as it can impact future development. Therefore, developmental milestones provide insight into skills children hold or ones they need to develop further, allowing for the children's village to monitor development.

All children develop in several areas from birth, with development increasing in complexity as they age. Categories of developmental milestones include movement/physical development, social/emotional, adaptive, language/communication, and cognitive, and each age has corresponding skills and tasks that demonstrate normal development (Center for Disease Control and Prevention, 2023). Also, skills within developmental categories can overlap. For instance, children that learn to grab objects may also stack those objects, thus utilizing both fine motor and cognitive skills to accomplish such tasks. According to Zubler et al. (2022), evidence-informed developmental surveillance tools demonstrate what normal young child development may encompass through five years of age. Examples of skills within each developmental category being mastered by five years old may include:

Movement/Physical: This category encompasses how children utilize their hands and move their bodies. Examples include holding crayons/pencils (not using fists), stringing items together, catching a large ball, sitting, walking, and running.

Social/Emotional: This category encompasses how children feel and behave, as well as how they relate to others. Examples include calming when picked up and comforted after a few minutes, comforting others, playing independently and/or with children, following rules/taking turns, singing/dancing, and naming basic feelings (happy, sad, mad, scared).

Language/Communication: This category encompasses how children understand and communicate language with others. Examples include having conversations with back-and-forth exchanges, talking well enough where others know what is being said, answering simple questions, talking about at least one event that occurred during the day, and saying their first name.

Cognitive: This category encompasses how children explore, learn, and think to problem solve. Examples include counting to 10; writing letters, names, and colors; and drawing a circle when shown.

Adaptive: This category encompasses life skills that carry out basic functions to act independently. Examples include putting clothes on by themselves, using eating utensils, washing hands independently, using the toilet independently, and lacing shoes.

Development during the early years is an arduous and complex process, with each skill building on the previous skills learned. Although some children may be delayed in one or more categories of development or have disabilities/limitations, they can still benefit from activities within this book to master the skill of self-regulation, as we all have the capacity to regulate big feelings.

Helping young children learn how to regulate emotions requires teaching self-regulation, consistently having them practice self-regulation, and modeling emotions and self-regulation for them. Hence children learn the skill of self-regulation through relationships and through developmentally appropriate avenues, such as play, connection, and creative activities.

Later in this book, we will discuss more in depth the concept of play regarding social-emotional development. The activities shared within this book will allow the trusted adult to assume the role of teacher and expert by assisting children in developing the skill of self-regulation.

CHAPTER 2

PLAY: CHILDREN'S SOURCE OF EMPLOYMENT

Play is the most important task that children will have and is connected to every arena of optimal development. This chapter will highlight different types of play and how essential play is for children to not only work toward developmental milestone achievement but to successfully master those milestones at their personal best. Milestones include, but are not limited to, reaching early learning capacities, academic achievement, problem solving, building lasting friendships, learning compliance and cooperation, and the important life task of building belief systems and empathy for the world. Together, these milestones are the building blocks for success in their current experiences and in their future years.

THE FUNCTION AND SERVICE OF PLAY

Though the findings of developmental theorists such as Piaget (1929, 1952, 1962) and Parten (1932, 1933) vary in terms of their understanding about children's development, they solidly agree on the importance of play to the role of the developing brain. Play is a key and essential component toward brain development and developmental functioning, including cognitive, adaptive language, motor, and social-emotional. When we observe children with intentionality, their play can reveal a great deal about their temperament, their growth areas, and their strengths.

Piaget's (1929, 1936) beginning theory of cognitive development viewed play as integral to the development of intelligence in children. His theory of development argues that as children mature, their environment and play should encourage further cognitive and language development. This theory of play and development enlists a call to action for adults to continue fostering spaces that swell with opportunities to learn through environmental exploration. Piaget (1936) describes the stages of cognitive development and functions of play (1962) as follows:

PIAGET'S STAGES OF COGNITIVE DEVELOPMENT AND PLAY

- **Sensorimotor stage (Ages 0–2):** During this first stage of development, infants and early toddlers learn about their world through repetitive sensory-related experiences with their own bodies, other people (caregivers, daycare providers, siblings), and other objects. Children at this stage may explore things through touching and investigating their own bodies (grabbing their feet or blanket, looking at their hand, grabbing your hands), learning through oral sensory information (putting things in their mouths or biting you), touching (moving, manipulating, hitting, throwing, or dropping objects), and being activated by different sounds (e.g., music) or stimuli (e.g., lights or colors).

- **Preoperational stage (Ages 2–7):** Young children beginning at this stage take the sensory part of play and begin to make symbolic meaning and mental representations of people (whether they are physically present or not), places, and objects. This is the stage when pretend play begins to occur. As children grow in this stage, they are still limited in thinking they are the center of the environment, but a growing curiosity of the environment activates a deeper thinking and wanting to know about the world around them. This is why children at this stage ask so many important questions!

- **Concrete operational stage (Ages 7–11):** Children in this stage of development have acquired the basic tenets of logic, rules, cooperation, and acceptance by peers. Children are trying to integrate the logistics and social parts of play, which is crucial for building relationships with peers. *Who* children are playing with become just as important as *what* they are playing at this stage.

- **Formal operational stage (Ages 12 and up):** Youth at this age can look beyond concrete and logistical information and begin thinking more abstractly, hypothetically, or conceptually. They may enjoy games and rules with more complexity, solidify interests in particular types of activities, and include considerations of values and culture when engaging in recreational activities.

PIAGET'S FUNCTIONS OF PLAY:

- **Functional Play:** This type of play involves learning to use and manage one's body and manipulate objects with your hands for amusement or self-directed goal. Over time, functional play demonstrates better coordination and understanding of the meaning and use of an object for the purpose of play (e.g., splashing water, driving a toy car, shaking a rattle).

- **Constructive Play:** Being able to use objects to create something meaningful is at the heart of constructive play. Children at this stage want to explore, test, and try. They will use their will and determination along with imagination and problem-solving skills to make sense of the world around them (e.g., building with blocks, art projects, and creating things). This often serves as a transition competency to more symbolic types of play.

- **Symbolic/Fantasy Play:** Using objects to have representational meaning (e.g., a blanket as a superhero cape or yarn as spaghetti) is the main goal of symbolic play. Young children who are engaging in symbolic or fantasy play can engage in "make believe," act out important social roles or norms within their family or community, and create worlds within their recreation. Within symbolic play comes gateways towards literacy, problem-solving, and mindsight, or the ability to understand the emotional state of self and others.

- **Games with Rules:** Structured play includes any type of play that requires specific steps and rules or boundaries; within structured play is practice around regulation, compliance, the understanding of rules, logic, order, and outcomes.

Mildred Parten's research (1932) on the types of play that contribute to the healthy development of adaptive and social-emotional skills are also still cited today. In her research, Parten (1932) identified six stages of play that are important for children to learn and develop necessary skills they carry into adulthood. Parten's six stages of play include:

- **Unoccupied Play (Birth to 3 Months).** The first stage of play begins right after birth! Unoccupied play does not look like "traditional" play, as children do not seem to be doing anything. However, at this stage, children play by moving body parts, looking at things and faces, and engaging in tummy time.

- **Solitary Play (3 Months to 2 Years).** Simply put, the second stage of play is when children entertain themselves with activities that are self-directed. Although some adults may feel concern that their little one is playing alone, this stage is crucial for helping children develop cognitive skills related to problem solving, pattern recognition, and self-awareness.

- **Onlooker Play (2 Years).** At the third stage, children are interested in the play of other children their age but do not join in; this play is the adult equivalent of "people watching." It helps children (and adults) learn from others, understand complex social rules, and engage in curiosity about the world around them.

- **Parallel Play (2+ Years).** At the fourth stage, children play next to other children with similar toys while remaining independent. Although children are not playing with each other, they are doing a slow-to-warm-up dance that helps them start to understand social exchanges. Thus, the biggest skills learned at this stage are sharing and reading social cues.

- **Associative Play (3 to 4 Years).** At this stage, children now begin to play as a group and shift focus from objects to playing with others. This stage allows for children to put the social skills they have been learning into practice while developing new skills such as teamwork and communication, as well as begin to understand boundaries.

- **Cooperative Play (4+ Years).** This final stage of play is when children often engage in imaginative or pretend play with others and take on specific roles such as playing house. This type of play helps children further understand social relationships and rules, sharing and turn-taking, and healthy expression of emotions.

Educators, practitioners, and developmental theorists have observed and identified additional forms of play that children partake in and are helpful in their developmental journey. These include *locomotor play* (play that allows a variety of movement like climbing, crawling, or tumbling), *rough and tumble play* (activities that require high energy, impact, and physical contact), *communication/social play* (tasks that necessitate active communication or support navigating social dilemmas), *dramatic play/role play* (engaging in the lived experience of other people, places, or things with use of costumes, props, or responsibilities), and exploratory play (the use of curiosity and discovery such as scavenger hunts). It is important to note that even as adults, we engage in all these forms of play when we do things such as people watch, look at a family photo album, or play sports. Play is crucial in helping develop and shape the social skills necessary for healthy relationships, but also important to help express our emotions, feel pleasure, and engage in relaxation. Thus, play is a developmental process in which skills are formed and the foundation for self-regulation skills set to be mastered.

THE BENEFiTS OF PLAY

When thinking of the outcomes and accomplishments we want for our children, the power of play toward reaching developmental dividends cannot be overemphasized. In fact, there's no such as thing as playing too much! Recreation provides many transformative portals that channel the needed capacities for developmental growth to occur. Therefore, play is the foundation and blueprint for children to learn and thrive in an ever-changing world.

Here are a few key benefits that child development research across disciplines finds in common about the benefits and developmental outcomes of play:

- Develops cognitive skills and processing of new information
- Activates the growth of the brain, particularly the frontal lobe, which holds executive-functioning capacities
- Lends to procedural learning, planning, and problem-solving abilities
- Provides portals of entry for self-motivation, determination, industry, and resilience
- Establishes the template for behavioral flexibility and the ability to adapt to age-appropriate change and transitions
- Teaches and provides practice for independence (handling age-appropriate tasks alone) and interdependence (being able to know when you need others and how to ask for what you need)

- Provides opportunity for taking risks and trying new things
- Develops social awareness, social reciprocity, and quality of social engagement
- Allows for the discovery and exploring of roles, hobbies, interests, and learning about relationships
- Provides a foundation for success in early learning and beyond
- Generates creativity and imagination
- Creates space for practicing interpersonal effectiveness (e.g., negotiation, problem solving, resolving conflicts, and teamwork)
- Allows for practicing effective prosocial and communication skills
- Teaches children how to engage in cooperation and compliance when needed
- Creates building blocks for confidence and self-esteem
- Opens learning about themselves and their place in the world
- Generates understanding, processing, and responding to emotions in a healthy way
- Builds co-regulation and self-regulation capacities

THE iMPORTANCE OF PLAY

We cannot stress the importance of including yourself in recreation and play. This is not only for the development of the children in your care, but also for your own sense of curiosity, exploration, wonder, and enjoyment of the world around you! Some of your first experiences in play may have been affirmative, while others inhibitory, serving as a barrier to how you understand the organic nature of what it means to play and learn. Your own experiences with your family of origin and school experiences may impact how you might understand the concept of fun and recreation. For instance, play may have been welcomed and celebrated, such as frequently having family game nights or engaging in after-school activities, such as sports or clubs. However, for others, play may have been something that was absent or unwelcomed during childhood or aligned with certain messaging such as "work hard, play later."

As we get older, the distance between us and the sacredness of play grows. However, adults must never forget to engage in play and to work toward lessening our fear of being impacted by the humility and splendor in returning to this foundational part of our lives. Play allows for time to stand still and for us to be present and feel the most alive. When we are present, we can be most attuned to ourselves, others, our feelings, and what else we long to actualize or apprehend. Research informs us of how play over the lifespan keeps our brains and spirits young and vibrant. As adults, when we play, we begin to activate and experience a particular therapeutic healing. Having our own hobbies, interests, and pleasurable activities allows us to relieve stress, regenerate new energy, and even enjoy a great mental or physical workout! More importantly, this space allows us to continue initiating, building, and maintaining intimacy and connection with others. Within this, the journey that play takes us on becomes way more important than its proposed dividends. Play is what keeps us in consistent connection with ourselves, others, and the world.

When children want to play with us, it is often presented as the most acute matter. This sense of urgency is rarely a tactic to distract, disengage, or disobey. Often, young children's eagerness around the matters of play shows us how important we are to them as they ask us into the most intimate parts of their world. Because play is the source of employment for them, we are allowing them to show us who they are, how resilient they are, and what they need our help with in the world. This is a sacred party for us to be invited to. Within this dynamic, we not only watch them play but join them in this play, as it teaches us not just about how to show up for them, but the work we must also do for the child inside of us.

The act of play is rarely trivial or inconsequential, but essential to the relationships we have with ourselves and the children in our care. When we can engage in play with children, we are able to see the world as they see it, which provides portals of understanding about their way of being and their behavior. The understanding of behavior posits the questions around what is happening with them and to them, in grave contrast to what is wrong with them and what they are doing. This framework of curiosity allows us to appreciate their lived experience, respect their positionality, and create pathways that allow for more effective communication, for young children to comply or attend to redirection, and for more opportunities to bond and connect. The more we can spend time in the relationship in understanding, the less caregiving stress we feel and the more appreciation and growth we can share.

In Chapter 4 there will be journal prompts for adults to engage in reflective practices within this book. These reflective activities will help strengthen connections and attunement with children. We hope the chapter just for adults will be a gentle push inspiring you to bring out the best in your relationship with yourself and others, continue to maintain the playful parts of yourself, and reconnect you with play in new ways!

THE CULTURE OF PLAY

Culture (what makes us who we are) **and context** (where we are) are familial to learning and play. This is paramount to understanding the inner workings of children. The incomparable work from developmental theorist Lev Vygotsky provides a sociocultural theory of cognitive development to further understand the context for which we learn. His work emphasizes that a child's learning and development is deeply embedded within the culture and social network that they live in or have been exposed to. In other words, children learn through being with us and being connected to their culture of origin.

Children need us to be with them. That when we play with them, we are engaging in the epic nature of being a team player! Honoring the unique culture and needs that children share through their play allows them to grow and flourish. One way that we can be there is in the space between where they are developing and their developmental potential (the zone of proximal development). The presence of a peer or a caring adult role is to assist, guide, encourage, and teach (not control) them new ways to reach where we need them to be and where they yearn to go. Play provides the largest windows of opportunity for children to not only learn within their cultural context but to learn the art and tasks involved in emotional and behavioral regulation.

In sum, when we let children be creative, imagine, and play, we are allowing them to use their brains in a variety of different ways that support their understanding of social expectations, social rules, social responsibility, and empathy. Within this space, knowing yourself is just as paramount to knowing the inner workings of children. It is connected to how well you will be able to understand them.

CHAPTER 3

SELF-REGULATION ACTIVITIES

This chapter includes 20 engaging activities to help build self-regulation skills in young children. Each activity will include the following:

- The purpose, goal, and developmental arc of the activity
- A list of materials needed to engage in the activity
- A detailed instructional guide on how to implement the activity (including helpful prompts)
- Additional tips for the village, and ways to implement different activities across settings

The primary goal of these activities is to build and enhance the relationship you have with your children or students. Another goal is for you to thoroughly enjoy yourself and simply spend time with them as well. To optimize the enjoyment part, here are a few ground parameters about how to use these activities.

PARAMETER #1: DEVELOPMENTAL GUIDANCE

No matter where you are in life, one of the most important things you need is support when you are stuck, unsure, or having a hard time with a new transition. This support means a great deal in taking steps in the right direction. This support does not always come from a "teachable moment," explicit direction, abrupt intrusion, or overshadowing but by way of a nurturing space to reflect and come to a healthy decision, which is how we understand developmental guidance. Originally coined by world-renowned infant-parent mental health specialist Selma Fraiberg to support parents in recognizing and responding to their children's physical and emotional needs, developmental guidance can be applied to any caregiving person. It means seeing someone's humanity, noticing their physical and/or emotional need, and helping in a way that allows them to stay in the center, feel safe with you, and learn from the experience of being with you in that moment. Therefore, you might need to offer your children or pupils developmental guidance during activities.

PARAMETER #2: HOW YOU SHOW UP

Navigating the hustle and bustle of the day can be a challenge, and things that happen around us (which may not be our own doing or something we have contributed to) can impact the way we want to show up with children. Our goal in these moments (although challenging) is to be as present and attentive as we can. This means what we say (content) and how we say it (process) matters. How we show up with our thinking, our movement, our listening, and our sense of what might be going on is highly influential in how you bring yourself to the activity and how the children or pupils understand and respond to what you are introducing to them. In chapter 4 (page 71), forms were created for your use to help with your journey of self-reflection. These forms are available as a guide to thinking about the content and logistics of the time you are spending with the child, developmental competencies met (an answer key is included), the deeper meaning of these activities, how you and the child felt during the activities, and the relationship with one another that is building and forming as a result of your time together. There are times when what you are doing and feeling is just as important—if not more important—to children. These nonverbal messages about how you are feeling are being seen and processed regardless of if we have verbalized our internal experience with those in our care. The great thing about relationships is that we always have opportunities to listen, repair, re-correct, and bring ourselves back to being attentive and present, which is often widely accepted with open arms.

PARAMETER #3: PRACTICE

Whenever we are introduced with a new idea or a new way of thinking, there is a tension point. This tension point is not a bad thing, but a space where our brain, body, and spirit (energy) are trying to align and take, process, and integrate new things. This can be a challenging task, and both children and adults need grace, space, and time to learn new things. The only way we can move toward success in our endeavors is the art of practice.

The activities that follow are designed to use multiple times, in a variety of different ways or settings, and will require effort. It is okay if the activity does not work exactly as it should the first or even second time. These are opportunities for you to learn more about you and the relationship you have with the children in your care. As you master different activities, you might spark new and more innovative ways to connect with the young people you care about!

We hope that you enjoy exploring, implementing, and reflecting on the activities provided in this chapter. Please enjoy and have lots of fun!

THE KEEPSAKE

Purpose of the Activity

The purpose of this activity is to support young children with transitions. Introductions to new people and places can be challenging (for both young children and the adults in their care) and elicit big feelings like worry, fear, or sadness. It's essential to provide a nurturing and supportive space during these important transitions of change with the unfamiliar. This activity can help support regulation by allowing young children to bring the important and familiar to the space until the new experience becomes part of their routine and internalized as not so new.

Materials Needed

 Box (any size)

 Crayons, markers, and/or stickers

 Construction paper

 Glue

 Tape

 Photographs of important family members (including pets)

 Any small object that is of importance to the child, such as a toy or small blanket

Instructional Guide

Step 1: Introduce the activity to the child by stating that you are going to be creating something they can take with them to new places and spaces to remind them of home. Set materials out on the table and place the box in front of the child.

Step 2: Allow the child to decorate the box as they wish using the crayons, markers, stickers, construction paper, glue, tape, or family photographs. While the child is decorating the box, you can comment on their decoration skills and offer materials. For example, you may state, "Wow, I love how you are coloring the box blue" or "Do you need any more glitter?" It is important to let the child lead in decorating and to be there as a means of support. If they want you to join in the decoration with them, jump in! However, assume the role of their assistant by letting them still lead in the decoration of the box.

Step 3: After you and the child have decorated the box together, provide developmental guidance by helping the child verbalize the important parts of home that they are putting into their box. Hold up a photo and ask the child, "Who is this important person that you are putting into the box?" Or, pick up a chosen object and say, "Tell me about this very special toy you plan to put in your box." During this step, allow the child space to share openly about who and what they are putting in the box and why. This showing and telling offers you essential information about the child, what they value, their interests, and what makes them feel safe.

Step 4: After putting important items into their box, collaborate with the child to decide on a safe and accessible place to keep it. During this excursion, offer the child nurturing statements such as, "This box is always here when you need it," or "Whenever you are feeling worried, scared, or sad, your special box will be here, and I will be here too."

Village Tips: It may also be difficult and stressful for caregivers when watching their children become upset with transitions, especially if it is transitioning to school/daycare. Therefore, caregivers can also co-create their own keepsake with the child to use when separation occurs or for times, they may feel overwhelmed, guilty, or sad. In addition, professionals can also turn this activity into a session ritual by reviewing the items at the start of an appointment to help navigate and normalize the transition.

TODAY'S WEATHER REPORT

Purpose of the Activity

The purpose of this activity is to lay a foundation for basic emotional identification. When we know what feelings are, we can understand them, communicate with them, manage them, and ask for help with those feelings when we need it! This activity allows opportunities for caregivers and teachers to grow in their attunement and assessment of young children's emotional experience at the start (or in other important transitions) of the day and collaborate on how best to support them. While adults grow in their awareness of the emotional experiences of their children, the child not only learns about basic emotions but is hopeful that you will hear them and trust that you can hold and help with those feelings as well.

Materials Needed

 Poster chart or cards of visual basic emotions/feelings (see page 70)

 Poster chart or cards of emotions/feeling words (You can purchase this or create your own.)

 A poster or card that reads, "I feel _____ today."

Instructional Guide

Step 1: Hang up the poster chart and cards on the front door of the classroom, on the kitchen fridge, on an easel, or wherever you would like. Introduce the activity to the child by stating that you would like to know how they are feeling today. Share how important feelings are and how important their feelings are to you.

Step 2: On the poster or card that reads, "I feel _____ today," prompt the child to fill in the blank about how they are feeling today. Based on the developmental needs of the child, they can use visual prompts to help them articulate their emotional experience and how they are feeling that day.

Step 3: After the child shares their emotional experience, it is important to validate that experience by stating, "Thank you so much for letting me know what you are feeling today."

Village Tips: Understanding the emotional temperature in the classroom, at home, or while out in the community can be immensely helpful in knowing how to best respond to the child, whether that is amending plans and schedules or understanding what both you and the child, the family, or classroom can manage. This allows for the adults to be flexible in their demands of the day, while children have the opportunity to respond to their environment at their best.

MiRRoR, MiRRoR

Purpose of the Activity

Have you ever noticed how much infants love mirrors and gazing at themselves? This is an early developmental activity in which they start to recognize faces and facial expressions. The purpose of this activity is to expand on that social and emotional development by helping children continue to learn emotional identification via modeling emotions and mirroring others' emotions. This allows children to build social awareness and empathy for others. They also simultaneously notice what emotions feel like within themselves.

Materials Needed

 Floor mirror or large mirror

 Costumes or clothing, such as scarves, hats, and shirts

 Random objects around the room (e.g., book, cooking utensil, phone)

Instructional Guide

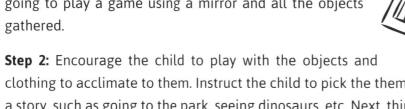

Step 1: Hang the mirror or lean it up against the wall. Gather all the costumes, clothing, and objects and lay them out so the child can see them all. Introduce the activity to the child by stating that you are going to play a game using a mirror and all the objects gathered.

Step 2: Encourage the child to play with the objects and clothing to acclimate to them. Instruct the child to pick the theme of a story, such as going to the park, seeing dinosaurs, etc. Next, think of a simple story to tell; feel free to be spontaneous and not worry too much about the plot.

Step 3: Use the objects and clothing to tell the story in the chosen theme while looking in the mirror together. While telling the story, create characters that feel happy, sad, mad, and/or scared to help the child start identifying feelings and seeing how feelings are expressed in others. As you tell the story with a specific emotion, make sure to use big facial expressions to highlight the emotion. For instance, if the "mad dinosaur" is stomping around in the park, you may use a frown, clenched teeth, and large and hard stomps to highlight how that emotion may be expressed in others. Continue to associate the characters with the same emotions so the child can internalize what those emotions are and what they look like within others.

Step 4: After the story is done, have the child act out the characters with you in the mirror so they can begin to understand how emotions are expressed and felt within them. For example, you may say, "Stomp like the angry dinosaur" or "Smile like the happy bird."

Village Tips: Mirrors can be integrated in various ways to continue to build on this developmental skill. For instance, a child can extend this activity while brushing their teeth and looking in the mirror. In the classroom or a professional setting, a child can talk to their reflection in a mirror, which will help them notice their facial expressions and emotions as they talk and play.

MY SACRED SPACE

Purpose of the Activity

When you are upset or have had a long stressful day, what do you do to manage? Often, adults say they "just need some space" or a "moment of peace," which may include taking breathing breaks, sitting in silence, or eating an enjoyable meal alone. Just like adults, children also need space to help them cool down big feelings (i.e., regulate) and bounce back from stress. The ability to take space helps us pause to calm down, recognize what we may be feeling, and think through how to respond to those feelings and stressors. This activity helps children begin to learn the skills necessary to self-soothe by using objects and things they find relaxing.

Materials Needed

 A designated space or corner of the room

 Comfy blankets and pillows

 Books

 Basket that may include bubbles, a small snack, crayons/markers, paper, and a stress ball

Instructional Guide

Step 1: Identify a designated space or corner and tell the child that you are going to create a space that is just for them to use when they have big feelings and need to cool down.

Step 2: Decorate the space with the blankets, pillows, books, and a basket of items, as well as any other nonelectronic objects they may find relaxing, such as stuffed animals.

Step 3: After you decorate the space, have the child sit and play in the space to acclimate themselves to it. Tell them that they can use this space any time they feel mad, sad, or scared.

Step 4: Practice directing the child to the space to learn how to use it when they have big feelings. For instance, if the child is having a temper tantrum/outburst, you can pick them up and sit in the space, holding them until they calm down, then engage in the surrounding items, such as books or bubbles. Several attempts may be needed before they understand how and when to use the space. Slowly titrate assisting them by placing them in the space alone and sitting outside the space, or placing the child in the space alone and standing a few feet away. The key is practice and consistency!

Village Tips: This activity is more challenging, as it requires lots of practice, consistency, and tolerating big emotions. As an adult, you can create your own sacred space too—you deserve it! You could even "show and tell" your space to the child and model using it, which would help them know we *all* need our own space to cool down. Additionally, this activity works well in a classroom setting as a way to help students take pauses during the school day.

KANGAROO COMFORT

Purpose of the Activity

Regardless of our age, we cannot completely escape from challenges, transitions, and stress. However, when we think about how we were able to navigate these intrinsic or environmental adjustments, we can often recall someone who brought emotional and physical comfort. This comfort felt meaningful and transformative because it was given in a way that we found to be affirmative; it was what we needed and asked for, not someone else's suggestion or desire for us. Support of this nature is often the launching station for resiliency, motivation, and determination to move forward in stressful situations. This activity offers help with handling and articulating big feelings.

Special Note: This is also a great activity in response to "Today's Weather Report" on page 30.

Materials Needed

 Poster board or portable cards

 Photographs or iconography that includes the following: a hug; a high five, fist bump, or special handshake; something plush/comforting; a moment alone in a safe space

Instructional Guide

Step 1: Take materials and assemble your board, with the photographs to the poster board or portable cards. You can designate a specific place for this board's location, whether outside of the classroom by the door, in your circle times space, or on the refrigerator if you choose to do this activity at home.

Step 2: When a child is experiencing a negative or difficult feeling (e.g., sadness, frustration, or worry) or wants to feel safe, provide a validation statement using one of the following prompts:

⭐ "I see that you are feeling _____ ."

⭐ "It's okay to feel _____ and I want to help/I want you to be safe."

⭐ "There are things we can do when we are feeling _____ ."

After letting them know how important feelings are and how important their feelings are to you, ask them about choices to help them in that moment. Then, use the photographs on the poster board or cards to introduce the choices that they have that can provide comfort to them.

Special Note: Used during the morning routine or other important transition times, this activity allows for caregivers and teachers to exchange helpful information about children's emotional needs and collaborate on how to best support them. You can implement this activity with these items posted wherever you like (e.g., the front door of the classroom, magnetized on the kitchen fridge, made portable to bring with you to a table or desk, etc.).

Step 3: With the materials provided, prompt the child to articulate what they need in response to their feelings or emotional experience. They can share their words or choose/point from the virtual options provided.

Step 3: After the child selects from their comfort contact choices, you can implement this right away by responding with their choice!

Step 4: After responding with their choice, feel free to check in with them on how they are feeling and let them know that you are there for them if they need more help with their feelings throughout the day!

Village Tips: Just like children, adults also need comfort and contact. The reflection sheets in Chapter 4 can be useful to help you reflect on what you may need in stressful moments. In addition, Kangaroo Comfort can be expanded on in the classroom by having students complete this activity as a group and then encouraging them to use it throughout the week.

TEACHER'S PET

Purpose of the Activity

One of the most noble and important responsibilities parents and educators have is that of caretaking—providing space for children's wellness and growth and allowing them to internalize how important they are. The act of caretaking births spaces where seeds of empathy and understanding of self, others, and togetherness can grow. This activity builds skills related to empathy, compassion, perspective taking, and sharing space in a fun way. It also provides a space for the child to engage in practicing what it means to take care of something important.

Special Note: This activity can be done with special tasks or with a real pet at school and home if there is already a real pet in those settings or with special tasks around home and school as well!

Materials Needed

 A plush animal (Make sure the animal has a name as well!)

 A box or clear bag

 A small blanket, washcloth, and toothbrush

 A small play-based food item (e.g., a plastic apple, banana, broccoli)

Instructional Guide

Step 1: Introduce the activity to the child by stating that you need their help with a very important thing you will show them. You want to build excitement about this important thing and gauge their interest.

Step 2: Introduce the plush animal as a "new pet" and mention how special it is. Allow the child to become acquainted with this new pet by touching, feeling, looking at, and holding it. This can also be a perfect time to provide developmental guidance around safe touch and handling things with special care.

Step 3: After the child becomes acquainted with the "new pet," introduce the idea of giving them a very special job: taking care of it at home (if this is a school activity) or taking care of the pet in their room or around the house (if this is home activity). Walk the child through the contents of the box or plastic bag, calling it the "caretaking box," and describe what the contents are for (e.g., a blanket for bedtime or naptime, a washcloth and toothbrush for bathtime, food for dinner/snack, etc.). Have the child repeat back some of the important items about caretaking that you shared with them.

Step 4: After introducing the above tasks, give them the box or bag to bring home or to their room for a day, a few days, a full week, or on an ongoing basis, depending on the developmental capacities of the child and what resources might be available to you to create this pet opportunity. The goal is not for the child to engage in perfect caretaking but for them to give connection, care, and affection to something outside of themselves.

THE POWER OF TOUCH

Purpose of the Activity

The five basic human senses are taste, smell, hearing, touch, and sight. In infancy, touch is the first sense to develop, as it is an innate need we all have. Touch contributes to physical and emotional functions, such as attachment and relaxation. Touch can help lower cortisol, release oxytocin (the "love hormone"), and enhance a secure attachment. Therefore, touch, along with the other senses, plays a vital part in self-regulation. Engaging in a child's sense of touch can be a playful way to help them utilize this sense to cope with big feelings such as anxiety or anger and help release pleasurable feelings such as relaxation.

Although touch is important and can be playful, it is also important to teach young children about safe touch and boundaries. The Committee for Children (2024), provides guides for all ages on how to have these important conversations. Search for the Hot Chocolate Talk® Campaign resource at https://www.cfchildren.org/resources/child-abuse-prevention/ and preview it before beginning this activity. This activity is to be used at home only given the consent and boundaries around touch. However, in the tips below are ways this can be expanded to classroom and professional settings. More importantly, during this activity, anytime the child says things like "No," "Stop," or "Done" (even when laughing), please immediately stop and ask for permission to begin the activity again. By respecting the child's wish to stop, this activity also helps the child learn about boundaries and consent, even when lots of giggles are happening!

Materials Needed

 Brush/comb

 Feather

 Lotion

 Paintbrush/makeup brush

 Something fuzzy or furry (e.g., a blanket, cotton ball, or stuffed animal)

Special Note: The most important material in this activity is YOU. Physical affection from you can be a powerful way to strengthen connection with children and help establish safety and security within the relationship.

Instructional Guide

Step 1: Tell the child that they are going to learn about different kinds of touch, including what kinds of touch they may like. This would be a great moment to then have the conversation about boundaries and safe touch.

Step 2: Begin using the materials one at a time to touch the different body parts they consent to. If you are using yourself as the material, you can use your hands to tickle them, provide hugs with various pressures, massage their feet or hands, and stroke or brush their hair. Be sure after each touch, you check in on how that touch felt for them. Ways to check in may include asking for a thumbs up/down or observing their body language and noting it aloud, such as "I see you smiled" or "I noticed you rolled away." As you engage in touch with different materials, also allow them to try them out on you. This can be another moment to model boundaries and consent for them around touch.

Step 3: After you have tried some of the materials, ask which ones they liked the best and least. Knowing this information can help you understand how to respond with touch to big feelings or tantrums. For instance, if the child noted the fuzzy socks were the best, when a future moment of distress occurs (e.g., crying or yelling), you can have them feel the socks with you to help use touch to provide relaxation and calmness.

> **Village Tips:** Caring for children is one of the most important, yet difficult, jobs. Therefore, it is important for adults to reflect on ways they enjoy being touched and cared for too, such as a hug from a partner or friend, snuggling with a favorite blanket, or massages. This activity can also be integrated to classroom and professional settings in the form of fist bumps or hand/clapping games such as Slide, Pat-a-Cake, or Rockin' Robin.

MINDFUL MUNCHING MUNCHKINS

Purpose of the Activity

Enjoying a tasty snack is a pastime for every age. Snack or mealtime is often communal and collectivistic in nature. We enjoy our food, socialize with our food, share food, and build awareness and relationships over food. The purpose of this activity is for children to build tolerance around gratification and enjoyment while taking notice of self, others, and what is in front of them. This activity can be done with an individual child, among siblings or cousins, in small groups at school, or with the entire classroom!

Materials Needed

 Plates

 Napkins

 Snacks

 Timer/stopwatch

 Child-friendly cleaning wipes

Special Note for Snacks: We want this to be both fun and easy to implement (and clean up). Finger foods are easy for young children to hold, manipulate, enjoy, and clean up! Some great examples of snacks for this activity include strawberries, blueberries, banana or orange slices, goldfish crackers, graham crackers, and cookies.

Instructional Guide

Step 1: Introduce the special snack time to your child or students. Share that part of what you will be doing today is playing with your snacks before you eat! Let them know that they must do four things with their snack to begin.

Step 2: Provide a napkin and plate to the child. If orange slices are today's snack, provide an orange slice on the child's plate. Give each of the following prompts:

 "Let's take a look at our snack."

☆ "Now, let's listen to our snack."

☆ "It's time to touch our snack now."

☆ "Let's smell our snack."

☆ "Let's taste our snack!"

Using the stopwatch, separate these activities by 10 seconds (for two- to three-year-olds) and 15 to 20 seconds (for four- to five-year-olds) to allow time for the child to engage in the prompt you are giving them. It is important to immerse yourself with them and model the expectation for each prompt. Show excitement and curiosity with your child to increase excitement and engagement. Children can be expected to need help along the way in this new activity. We want to warmly redirect them back to the task and show them what they should be doing with you and/or with you and the group.

Step 3: Repeat the content in the second step two or three times. This is heavily dependent on the capacities of the child and/or group. After a few rounds, allow the children to enjoy the remainder of their snack without restrictions.

Step 4: After enjoying the special snack, each child can be given an extra napkin and sanitation wipe. With prompting from you, they can clean their place, dispose of any waste, and clean their hands and faces.

STOP AND SMELL THE COOKIES

Purpose of the Activity

As mentioned in "The Power of Touch" on page 40, sensory experiences are a powerful way to help with self-regulation. When children are experiencing big feelings or are overstimulated, helping them come back to the present moment using their senses is crucial. Indeed, our sense of smell is *the* most powerful tool we have to immediately connect us back to the present moment when feeling overwhelmed. This concept is known as "grounding" and helps with self-regulation since it allows children to remove themselves from intense feelings or overstimulation quickly in the moment.

Materials Needed

 See: Identify three things around the room

 Feel: Gather two things to feel, such as a fuzzy blanket or touch book

 Smell: Gather one thing to smell, such as scented lotion or a baked good like cookies

Instructional Guide

Step 1: This activity is best taught when the child is feeling relaxed and playful. Introduce the activity by telling them that you are going to play a game using their eyes, hands, and nose that will help them when they have big feelings and need to cool down.

Step 2: To best understand the power this activity has in regulating emotions and overstimulation, engage the child in a physical activity to increase their heart rate. For instance, you can have them hop for 25 seconds or run back and forth or in a circle for a minute.

Step 3: After the physical activity, tell the child to stand still (or you can hold them), look around the room, and ask what three things they see around the room. If they have a hard time finding three things, you can help them identify things within the room. Next, ask the child to feel the two things you've gathered. As they feel each one, ask them, "How does this thing feel?" or "Does it feel smooth or bumpy?" Lastly, ask the child to smell one thing, such as lotion or cookies. Of course, if they want to eat the cookie after they smell it, they can! You can ask them how it feels on their tongue.

Step 4: After you go through all the things to see, feel, and smell, you should notice their heart rate decrease and their body become a bit more relaxed. It is best to practice this a few times when the child is relaxed and playful before trying to implement it when they are having big feelings or overstimulated. When they are in distress (e.g., crying, screaming, hitting), you can hold them and do the activity together. Feel free to repeat until you notice their feelings and bodies cool down and they become grounded to the present moment.

Village Tip: This technique also works for adults when feeling overwhelmed. Practice using your favorite scents, especially when caring for children becomes stressful. This activity can be expanded by having diffusers to enhance calmness/relaxation or doing this activity as a group reset after a transition period such as recess or lunch.

RESONATION STATION

Purpose of the Activity

Adults often forget using their own voices to make necessary noise. Taking up good space is something that young children do an amazing job with daily. Their level of curiosity, wonder of the environment, and attempts at finding their connection to others and their world are quite brilliant. This brilliance can often be misunderstood as noncompliance or in direct conflict with adult agendas. The purpose of this activity is not only to create intentional spaces to make noise and move your body but to help children understand their body-earth connection while by themselves or with others. This activity will help support this connection with sounds, beats, and rhythms. The understanding of the body is the prerequisite for regulation, compliance, and being able to both follow and lead during interpersonal interactions.

Materials Needed

 Instrumental music (This could be played from your smartphone or on another music player device.)

 Drums (Styrofoam cup), drumsticks (child-friendly plastic spoons), flat and open table or floor space

 You, your body, and your best dance moves

Instructional Guide

Step 1: Introduce the activity to the child as a time when everyone will get to move their body in fun ways. Let them know you will guide them through different ways to move their body during the activity. This activity can be done at a table, on the floor/carpet, or standing!

Step 2: Choose sounds, beats, or rhythms, or a combination of the three. Your child will follow your lead in a gradual way, and that is perfectly okay!

 Sounds: You can use music or yourself to produce different sounds. This could be nature sounds, animal sounds, or a creation of your own sounds! Have the children try to repeat the sounds that they hear.

Beats: Use yourself (and materials you have listed above) to demonstrate different beats with gradual complexity. For example, you can begin by a tap on the table, then two taps, then three, then lots of taps. You can also engage in intervals of loud tapping/drumming to soft drumming.

 Rhythms: Play music and provide age-appropriate movements or dance moves (e.g., swaying back and forth, bending knees up and down, making shapes with arms, etc.).

Separate these by 10 seconds (two- to three-year-olds) and 15 to 20 seconds (four- to five-year-olds) to allow time for the child to engage in the prompt you are giving them. It is important to immerse yourself with them and model the expectation for each prompt. Show excitement and curiosity with your child to increase excitement and engagement. Children are expected to need help along the way in this new activity. Warmly redirect them back to the task and show them what they should be doing with you and/or with you and the group.

Step 3: Repeat the content in the second step for two to three rounds. This is heavily dependent on the capacities that the child and/or group can handle. After a few rounds, allow the child some time for a dance or movement break (20 to 30 seconds) to release any needed movement and prepare for reengagement. It is strongly encouraged for adults to join in the party!

Step 4: After engaging in the activity, implement a more calming or cooling down activity to help with regulation and transition to the next activity or task for the day. For example, taking a water/bathroom break, transitioning to lunch or snack time, naptime, or reading time would be great transitions here!

Village Tips: Movement is beneficial for adults and children! Having dance parties at home, enrolling in sports activities, or signing up for a yoga/fitness or dance class outside of work-home-school related spaces can be beneficial in creating intentional spaces to move your body, learn how you use your body in intentional ways, and alleviate stress!

TiP OF THE iCEBERG

Purpose of the Activity

This activity is great when the child is experiencing intense emotions such as anger or sadness or when the emotions are leading to potentially harmful behaviors such as hair pulling or head banging. Temperature is a quick way to pull ourselves out of intense feelings we experience. Have you ever been annoyed or frustrated and stated, "I just need to get some fresh air?" This activity employs a similar concept to what we adults engage in to cool down our feelings. Since children don't have that privilege to step outside on their own, this activity will help the child immediately cool down big feelings by utilizing something cold, and this activity can be done anywhere.

Materials Needed

 Two ice cubes

 Small ziplock bag

Instructional Guide

Step 1: Place two ice cubes in a small ziplock bag to create a cold pack. Introduce the activity to the child by stating that you are going to be feeling and playing with something cold and that they can use something cold when they feel mad or sad. Next, talk to them about specific moments when they felt mad or sad. In addition, if they are having a hard time finding moments they felt mad or sad, you can share moments you felt mad or sad and help highlight moments you may have also noticed them feel sad or mad.

Step 2: Next, let the child play with the ziplock bag of ice cubes. You can toss it back and forth and make a game such as hot potato. After they become familiar with the cold pack, put the cold pack aside and tell them to hop or jump for 20 seconds to increase their heart rate. For children five and above, you can also tell them to think of something that makes them mad as they get their heart rate up.

Step 3: After they increase their heart rate, give them the cold pack to hold. This should immediately decrease their heart rate. Practice this several times and try putting the cold pack on different body parts such as the hands, head, neck, or arm.

Step 4: The real practice comes into play when the child *actually* experiences extreme and intense feelings. Therefore, make sure to have a cold pack on hand to help tip the child's emotions back to a state of calmness.

Village Tips: This activity also works for adults, especially when you can't escape a situation or environment! When feeling overwhelmed or stressed in the moment, you can also grab something cold such as ice water or a fan to help tip you back to a state of calmness.

THE TALKING STICK

Purpose of the Activity

Language and communication skills are salient during the early developmental period. We want to provide every opportunity possible for young children to demonstrate verbal ability and engage in meaningful conversation. The access to these opportunities builds capacities not only for understanding language and providing language to others, but for basic social communication, reciprocity, and understanding the importance of having meaningful relationships. The purpose of this activity is to provide a space for children to begin engaging in self-expression, waiting their turn, and allowing for others to take up space and protect themselves, while also maintaining relationships within the group (whether in the classroom or at home).

Materials Needed

 Construction paper

 Markers or crayons

 Stickers

 Paper towel roll

 Scotch tape

Instructional Guide

Step 1: Before introducing this activity, create your talking stick with the child as a prerequisite to the activity. Allow the child to decorate the construction paper using the markers or crayons. If this is in a group, allow each student or child to place a sticker anywhere they want on the construction paper. Cover the paper towel roll with the decorated paper, then use the Scotch tape to laminate the talking stick for durability and multipurpose use!

Step 2: During a group setting like a family meeting, mealtime at home, or circle time in the classroom, introduce the talking stick as a special tool that will help you to talk and share your thoughts and feelings. You can share how important everyone's voice is and express how you want to make sure that you can hear from each person by saying, "To make sure everyone has a chance to talk, we will use the talking stick. If you are holding the talking stick, it is your turn to share, and if you do not have the talking stick, it is your turn to listen." Feel free to share these instructions multiple times and in different ways so that your child can internalize the goal of the talking stick.

Step 3: After you've shared the rules around the talking stick, practice using it by implementing a topic that is age appropriate and easy to share. An example of a topic is children's favorite things (e.g., color, toy, snack, or movie, etc.). You can expound on this as the child's capacity to take on the talking stick method grows. Children are expected to need help along the way in this new activity. Warmly redirect them to the task and show them what they should be doing with you and/or with you and the group.

> **Village Tip:** You can also facilitate this as an art activity in the classroom, where students can create their own talking stick. Families can be prepped on the nature of this activity and be encouraged to practice the use of the talking stick at home.

OUT OF THE BOX

Purpose of the Activity

Most of a child's day is organized and led by the adults in their lives. This can often result in a limited range of time and space for young children to practice true and virtuous creativity and exploration, which could steer them toward their own problem-solving capacities. These problem-solving capacities lay the foundation for future leadership skills. Within leadership, we find courage, articulation of wants and needs, the ability to learn from mistakes, and teamwork. The purpose of this activity is for young children to build creativity and leadership capacities while the caring adults learn what it is truly like to be in the position of a learner.

Materials Needed

 Cardboard boxes of various sizes/lengths (This could also include empty paper towel or toilet paper rolls.)

 Jumbo markers

 Masking tape (of various colors)

Stopwatch or timer

Instructional Guide

Step 1: Introduce the activity to the child, informing them that there is an important mission to complete. You can create any scenario or mission. Here are some examples of potential ideas for missions:

 A star is lost in space, and we need to find it.

 A baby sea otter is stuck in the coral reef, and their parents need our help to get them out.

 A family of jumping frogs needs our help finding a new home to live in.

The goal is to find a way to help. Say, "We need a leader to help us create or build something that will help us save the day!" Identify the leader and prompt them to be in charge. You want to provide every encouragement you can to build their self-esteem and orient them to being in charge, with you along with any others in the group being there to listen and follow their directions!

Step 2: Set the materials out on the table or floor in front of the child. You can share that you have 15 minutes (or whatever time you have available) for your mission. Say, "On your mark, get set, it's time to take the lead!" During this step, offer developmental guidance to the child and the group to orient them to the task. This may likely be the first time that they have ever been in charge. Part of the task for the adult in this step is watch and wonder with your child as they embark as the leader in this activity.

Step 3: Allow the child to take the lead and provide instructions on how to use the boxes, cardboard pieces, and other materials to create something that will help with the mission. The goal is not to critique or guide, but to listen and take instructions/feedback. Do not provide any feedback about how they are leading or how you think it could have gone better, as you are only there to help when asked or if there is a need to reestablish safety. Encourage them to make a choice, clarifying you are there to follow their rules.

Step 4: After the child has completed the mission or the time has run out, provide lots of praise for the completion of their mission or efforts of getting close. Praise (and not feedback or criticism) is paramount in this activity. You want to continue building courage, motivation, and hope that they can take on challenging tasks, solve age-appropriate problems, and ask for help when needed. There will be plenty of time to practice and refine leadership capacities at another time.

Village Tips: If this is in a group or classroom setting, you can repeat steps and allow each child to take their turn leading this expedition. You can also assign a leader for daily or weekly missions!

MY LiTTLE CookBook

Purpose of the Activity

If you have ever tried to put together a piece of furniture, you know the importance of following the directions. The last thing you want is to have to take it apart just to put it back together! Learning how to follow directions is an important skill for younger children, as it helps them learn and engage in problem-solving skills. Problem-solving skills are especially important as they start to navigate peer relationships and enter new environments such as school or daycare. Ultimately, problem-solving skills help them to independently handle future stressful situations and feelings as well as become adults who follow directions to put even the most challenging furniture configurations together!

Materials Needed

 Paper

 Markers

 Tortilla

 Cheese (e.g., chihuahua, cheddar)

 Tomato (already diced)

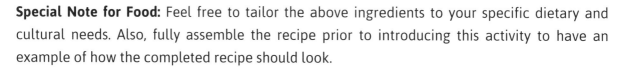

Special Note for Food: Feel free to tailor the above ingredients to your specific dietary and cultural needs. Also, fully assemble the recipe prior to introducing this activity to have an example of how the completed recipe should look.

Instructional Guide

Step 1: Introduce the activity to the child by stating that you are going to be creating a cookbook with them and the first recipe will be making a quesadilla. Place the quesadilla on the table. As you talk about creating the cookbook, this could be a great time to talk about what their favorite foods are, ones they want to add to the cookbook, and any questions they may have about food or the activity. Also, it could be fun to have them taste all the ingredients independently before assembling to encourage food exploration!

Step 2: Gather all the materials and lay them out on the table. Begin by using the markers and paper to make a numbered list that consists of three or less steps to follow. The directions should be short, as the goal is helping them learn how to follow simple step directions. As they increase in age, you can always add more steps and details. For this activity, your steps may read as follows:

1. Add cheese to tortilla.

2. Sprinkle tomatoes.

3. Fold tortilla.

Step 3: Next to each step, draw and color a simple visual representation of the step with them. For instance, for "sprinkle tomatoes" you may simply draw a tomato and have them color it.

Step 4: After you have drawn pictures and steps, complete the steps together to assemble the quesadilla. Once it is completed, ask them to make one for you. The goal is for them to eventually learn how to follow steps independently, but you may have to redirect them to the step or help them figure out what step is next. Again, practicing following the steps will help them develop their problem-solving abilities.

Step 5: Heat the quesadilla up in a pan and enjoy a meal together!

Village Tips: This activity helps to acclimate young children to following simple visual and written instructions. This activity can be expanded to professional and classroom schedules via visual schedules or instructions. Additionally, as you create future recipes, you will learn how short and clear directions need to be in order for the child to make sense of them. For instance, adults often say things such as, "Don't play at the table," which does not actually communicate what behavior we want to see the child demonstrate. Instead, a more clear statement may be, "Use your fork for eating." Therefore, this activity also helps adults understand how to communicate directions clearly, which ultimately helps set the stage for young children to learn how to engage in problem-solving skills.

LET THE SHOW BEGIN!

Purpose of the Activity

As adults, we enjoy compliments and positive feedback about things we do well—it *temporarily* boosts our mood and self-esteem. However, during moments of stress or negative feelings such as embarrassment, external feedback and compliments may not be readily available to help us cope. In such cases, coping with big emotions sometimes requires the ability to engage in positive self-talk to decrease the intensity of the feeling. For instance, think of a time that you failed at something such as an exam or meeting a deadline and felt deeply embarrassed. You may have coped with that situation and feeling by using positive self-talk, such as "This setback does not define me," and that positive statement and reframe likely helped to decrease the intensity of the negative feeling you experienced in the moment. Likewise, the purpose of this activity is to celebrate your child's strengths and talents by showering them with compliments to temporarily boost their mood and receive positive feedback, as well as give them space to start identifying their own strengths and talents to cope with future negative feelings to begin their development of positive self-talk.

Materials Needed

 Glitter

 Stickers

 Poster or poster board

 Markers

Special Note for Materials: Depending on your child's chosen talents, you may need to gather other materials beforehand.

Instructional Guide

Step 1: Introduce the activity to the child by stating that they will put on a talent show and make a poster for it. Explain to them what a talent is, such as "something they are really good at." As the adult, you can even model a talent of yours for them. Also, ask them who they want to come to the show. You can even create personalized invites.

Step 2: Identify a "stage" for the talent show, such as a specific room, rug, or blanket on the floor. Next, use the materials to create a poster with the talent show sign. Let the child choose what they want the show to be called and allow them to decorate the banner any way they choose.

Step 3: Ask the child what talents they are thinking of performing at the show, and make a list. If they want to write out their talents, you can also have the child fill in the sentence stem: *I am really good at* _____. If they have trouble coming up with talents or strengths, you can also help them identify some by stating, "You know how to sing all your ABC's. What about that one?" After you have the list of talents, decorate the stage with the banner, and invite guests. Have the guests get comfy, and let the show begin!

Step 4: While the child is performing their talents, make sure to offer plenty of smiles, cheers, and claps to encourage and celebrate their strengths. After the show, check in with them about how it felt to show off what they are good at and who they want to invite to the next show.

> **Village Tips:** Hopefully, this activity also helps to reflect on unique strengths that you hold and how you use those strengths to contribute to caring for children. Additionally, this activity can be great for a classroom setting in which other children can see and recognize strengths in others.

HEaR Me RoaR

Purpose of the Activity

To engage in a solution, you first must know what the problem is. Children have the capacity and ability to identify emotions when they are as young as three years of age! Indeed, one of the core pieces of self-regulation is emotional identification. Therefore, to be able to manage big feelings a child experiences, they must *first* understand what that feeling even is! The purpose of this activity is to begin helping the child identify basic emotions through games, such as charades, to help them gain the foundational skill needed for self-regulation.

Materials Needed

 Construction Paper

 Scissors

 Markers

 Two bowls

Instructional Guide

Step 1: Tell the child that they are going to play the game of charades with you, and that they get to make the game with you. If they ask what charades is, you can explain it to them in simple terms such as, "It is where I will pretend to be something, and you have to say what I am." Then, demonstrate an example for them such as meowing (e.g., cat) and ask, "What Am I?" Hopefully, they will laugh and say kitty, cat, or your family pet's name.

Step 2: Next, let the child pick out the color of paper they want to use. Cut pieces of construction paper into eight medium-size squares. On four squares, you will draw with them a happy face, a sad face, a mad face, and a scared face. This is a good time to talk about times they may have felt those emotions, as well as ask them to act out that feeling. For instance, you can ask, "What face do you make when you are mad?" or "What do you do when you are mad?" On the other four squares, you will draw four animals, such as a dog, cat, bunny, and lion, and write the names of the animals underneath the drawings.

Step 3: After you have created four feeling faces and four animals, you are ready to play charades! Put the four feeling faces in one bowl and the four animals in the other bowl. When you are ready to play, take out one feeling face card and one animal card and begin acting the combination out. For example, you may take out the feeling card of "mad" and the animal card of "dog" and then act out a "mad dog" by stomping around the room and barking.

Step 4: Continue playing until all the cards have been used and for as many rounds as you wish! Once the child can name and understand basic emotions, you can always add more feelings and animals to the game to expand their ability to identify emotions. If you notice that a child is having a hard time identifying the emotion, you can always give them the answer and pause to model different ways that emotion can be expressed. For instance, for the feeling "happy," you may model it by smiling, jumping up and down, squealing or squeaking, or saying a phrase you hear them say, such as "Yay," when you know they are happy.

Village Tips: Sometimes adults also struggle to identify feelings! Plenty of times we recognize the feeling in our bodies but struggle to give a name to it. That may be because we feel tons of feelings throughout our lifetime, and we are constantly learning new ones. Therefore, utilizing a feeling wheel may help to expand learning about feelings together with your child or with a group, such as a classroom or therapeutic group. On page 60 is a tool called a "feelings wheel" that you can use to help guide this feeling exploration!

FEELINGS WHEEL

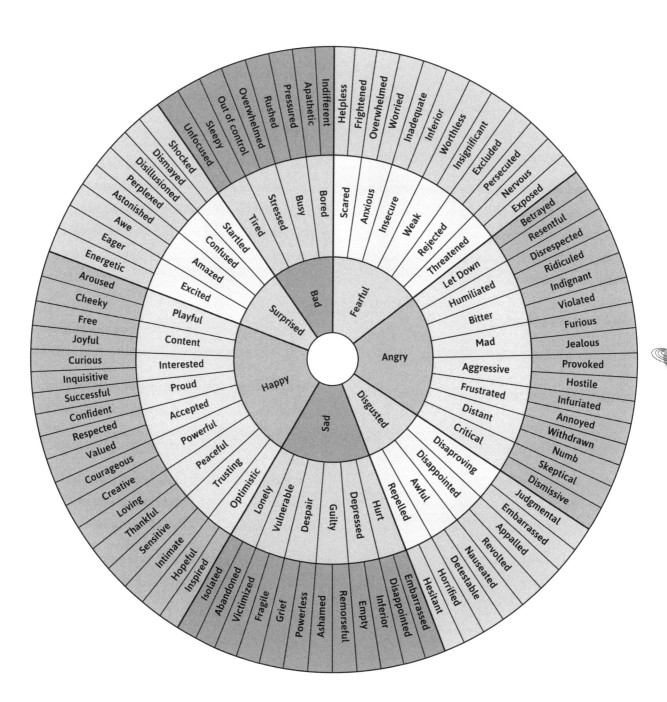

  THE SELF-REGULATION WORKBOOK FOR 3- TO 5-YEAR-OLDS

MIND READER

Purpose of the Activity

Young children are inherently self-centered, as they do not initially consider others' beliefs or feelings—this is developmentally appropriate. Rather, they must learn to understand others through social interactions. Theory of mind is a social-cognitive skill that helps us predict what another person may be thinking or feeling, which then helps us know how to respond. For example, if a friend is crying, you may guess that they are feeling sad and thus may offer a hug or some tissue. Therefore, theory of mind helps us to engage in positive social interactions and solve conflicts with others. It is important to note that some children with neurodevelopmental disorders such as autism spectrum disorder (ASD) have difficulties with this skill. However, with appropriate support and treatment, they can also learn it. The purpose of this activity will be to build theory of mind, specifically focusing on helping a child learn what another person may be feeling in the moment.

Materials Needed

 Feeling face cards (see page 70)

Instructional Guide

Step 1: Introduce the activity to the child by stating that they will play a feeling-guessing game in which you will read a story to them, and they have to guess what the animal is feeling.

Step 2: Have the child color and cut out the feeling face cards. If you want to expand this activity, you can also print out real faces of children displaying those emotions. You can google "sad face child" or "happy face child" to print out more realistic face cards.

Step 3: Once the face cards are completed, you are ready for story time. Tell the child you are going to read them a story and then they must guess what the animal is feeling by picking the feeling face card. Below are some stories you can read to help them guess what the feeling is. If you notice them having a hard time identifying a feeling, you can help them by highlighting the behavior the animal is doing (e.g., crying, stomping, yelling, etc.) within the story.

1. There was a little black cat named Cosmo, whose favorite food was milk. Every time he drank the milk, he would have a huge white milk mustache on his soft black fur. Today, his mom gave him some milk for a special treat, and he had the biggest smile! What do you think Cosmo was feeling?

2. Luna is a little gray bunny, and today is their first day of school. When Luna's dad takes them to school, Luna starts to cry lots of tears because they do not know any other bunnies. What do you think Luna may be feeling?

3. Wilbur was a huge lion who had the biggest roar in the jungle! One day Wilber was walking through the jungle with her friends and a tree tumbled down and almost fell on her. Wilbur jumped so high, let out the biggest roar, and showed her teeth. What do you think Wilbur may have been feeling?

4. Nova was a gorilla who loved to roll around on the floor and play with his favorite green drum. One day, Nova was rolling around and singing with his favorite drum when another gorilla took it from him. Nova stomped hard all over the floor and yelled at the other gorilla. What do you think Nova was feeling?

Step 4: After you have read all the stories and matched the feeling face cards, you can also expand this activity to the child's favorite books and ask what the characters may be feeling and thinking to continue to build this skill and increase their understanding of others' thoughts and feelings.

SAANVI SAYS

Purpose of the Activity

Taking initiative (leading) and waiting for steps toward initiating a task (listening) is a necessary regulatory capacity toward not only social-emotional development but ongoing learning at home and at school. The purpose of this activity is to provide your child with the opportunities to lead, listen, and take turns in a fun and engaging way!

Materials Needed

 Softball or ring (optional)

 Cards with animals or yoga poses (optional)

 Music (optional)

 You, your body, and your best dance moves

Instructional Guide

Step 1: Introduce the activity by sharing that you will be playing a very important game. Explain that you will be taking turns (whether this is a dyad, small group, or large group setting) taking the lead and listening with your eyes, ears, and body! After clarifying the instructions, introduce the game with whoever is starting first and calling it, " _____ Says." It is perfectly alright if you start as the "leader" to demonstrate how the game or task is to be done.

Step 2: For this step, you can choose mimicking, mirroring, or poses/movements. You can also choose a combination of them as well. This can be done in a relay format (in a line), with one person in front of the group, or with a circle and the leader in the middle:

 Mimicking: Use a ball or ring for a movement and then pass it to the next person, who will repeat the movement, and then pass the ball down the line until everyone in the line or circle has completed the task. For a dyad or triad, you can choose to do this round a couple of times or take turns each time.

 Mirroring: From the animal cards, the child can choose an animal to act out. The group can then try their best to mirror exactly how the leader portrayed the animal.

 Poses and movements: Use yoga poses or allow the child to choose an age-appropriate movement or dance moves (e.g., swaying back and forth, bending knees up and down, making shapes with arms, etc.).

Separate into different rounds with small breaks in between to allow time for the child to engage in the prompt you are giving them. It is important to immerse yourself with them and model the expectation for each prompt. Show excitement and curiosity with your child to increase excitement and engagement. Children are expected to need help along the way in this new activity. Warmly redirect them back to the task and show them what they should be doing with you and the group.

Step 3: You can repeat the content in the second step for several rounds. This is heavily dependent on the capacities of the child and group. After a few rounds, allow the child some time for a dance or movement break (20 to 30 seconds) to release any needed movement and prepare for reengagement. We strongly encourage adults to join in this activity!

Step 4: After engaging in the activity, a more calming or cooling-down activity is important to implement to help with regulation and transition to the next activity or task for the day. For example, taking a water/bathroom break, transitioning to lunch or snack time, naptime, or reading time would be great transitions here! You can also use this as a recess or outside activity as well!

ONCE UPON A TIME

Purpose of the Activity

Storytime is not just a nostalgic pastime that includes closeness, bonding, and preparation for a nap or bedtime; it is also an opportunity to increase literacy, comprehension, social awareness, and basic attending skills. Our ability to be motivated, encouraged, and responsive to various kinds of learning is very much connected to our early experiences and exposure to reading and literacy. The purpose of this activity is to help young children's attending, listening, and comprehension skills in a fun and engaging way. Another purpose of this activity is to build a growing understanding of transitions (that things have a beginning, middle, and end), empathy (identifying important characters and what they are navigating), and social awareness (what is happening in the story).

Special Note: This activity will be most beneficial in a dyadic or small group setting (no more than three little ones). This way you will have time and space to provide any needed developmental guidance throughout the activity.

It is important to slow down the process of traditional story time to create a more immersive experience for the developing child!

Materials Needed

 A comfortable space or area to sit

 Children's books (These can be traditional age-appropriate books you would find in a classroom; we also have some recommendations in our chapter on resources as well!)

 Laminated cutouts of images (or printouts taped/glued to an index card) that are replicated images in the book (e.g., If there is a tree on the page, a small cutout of a tree.) (optional material)

- This option might allow the activity to be more fruitful with younger children who are just recently building expressive and receptive language skills (two- to three-year-olds) or with children who have language/communication challenges.

Instructional Guide

Step 1: Gather the group to a comfortable space or area to sit. Introduce the activity as a "special story time." You can share that you are going to read a story together, but you will need their help in remembering and noticing important things that you will read.

If you are using the replicated cutouts, you can provide all of them to the child (if in a dyad) or a few to each child (if in a group). Lay them out in front of the children and help them in labeling what they see in front of them. You can explain that if they see any of these things while reading the story, they should hold it up and show you where it is on the page.

Step 2: When everyone is ready to engage in the activity, begin reading the story. Take your time reading, with some type of immersive task during the majority of the pages in the story. (Later steps include prompts to think about how to facilitate the immersive portion of this story.)

If you are using cutout images for your story time, please give intentional pauses to allow the child to notice and match their image with that in the story. If that child needs further developmental guidance, you can provide the following prompts:

 Do you see what you have in front of you or in your hand on the page?

 I see something red on the page. Do you have something red too?

If you are providing verbal information for your immersion portion of storytelling, the following are examples of prompts that can be helpful or useful to engage the children or group:

⭐ *I notice two things that are green on this page. Can you show me?*

⭐ *What's the name of the girl in the story?*

⭐ *What do you think will happen next?*

⭐ *How do you think that person feels in the story?*

⭐ *Can you help me remember what has happened in the story so far?*

Step 3: At the end of the story, be sure to praise the children or the group for their efforts in engagement in the story. It is less important to focus on what they were unable to do than what they accomplished during the activity. This is also a great time to review the story and learn about what the children or group remembers about the story. You can provide any needed encouragement to let them know that there will be plenty of additional opportunities to read and participate in more story time activities just like this one!

FEEL THE RaiNBow

Purpose of the Activity

One of the most important tools for development, ongoing learning, and life navigation is becoming an expert at one's own feelings. This growing expertise is the cornerstone for self-regulation and is heavily rooted in social-emotional intelligence. We need this form of intelligence throughout our lives and in almost every situation we encounter. Children may not know the name of feelings, but this does not mean that they do not have them, experience them, or notice when others are having them. Part of our role as caring adults is to help put a name to those emotional experiences. Knowing what big feelings are and when they are feeling that given experience is key for children to be able to manage it. The purpose of this activity is to build age-appropriate emotional identification capacities through associations with additional concrete knowledge.

Materials Needed

 Feelings cards (It is important that the cards you have include the "big six" feelings: happy, sad, mad/angry, surprised, scared/worried, and disgusted.) (See page 70.)

 Buckets or containers of various colors (You can also use construction paper of different colors, folders, or another other type of material with a solid designated color.)

Instructional Guide

Step 1A: Prior to implementing this activity, use the feelings cards and focus on six to ten emotions with color associations. Practice naming and acting out feelings with your child as a prerequisite activity before proceeding with additional steps.

Step 1B: After becoming more acquainted with feelings, you can introduce another step, which is connecting a feeling with a color. Have the child practice identifying the feeling and its color association.

Step 1C: Introduce the activity by sharing that you will be playing a special game to learn about feelings and that you will need their help! Share that you will give them a feelings card and you want them to place it on the color it belongs.

Step 2: After practicing step one as a prerequisite activity, you can provide them a feelings card, and they can provide at least one of the following based on their developmental capacity:

Verbalize what emotion is on the card;

 Show you the feeling by acting it out; OR

⭐ Place it in the correct color container.

Feel free to help support the child, but only after you have noticed that they have been given the space to problem-solve and have verbalized wanting your support and help. You can elect to navigate through this activity in several rounds and increase or decrease the range of difficulty based on developmental needs.

Step 3: After completing the card and color assortment, be sure to praise the child for their accomplishments and efforts. Provide guidance around those feelings cards that might have been placed in a different box than they belong. You can also provide encouragement by letting them know there will be lots of other times to practice learning more about feelings!

FEELINGS CARD

HAPPY

SAD

MAD

SURPRISED

SCARED

DISGUSTED

CHAPTER 4

REFLECTIVE SHEETS FOR ADULTS

At the beginning of this book, we highlighted how important you are to your children, students, or those in your care. This chapter is designed with you in mind, providing a space for you to take some time for yourself to engage in reflection and self-growth. We know and understand how busy a life taking care of children can be. The job of parents, teachers, and other forms of caregivers are invaluable to our neighborhoods, schools, and communities.

We cannot thank you enough for your time, effort, and caretaking of some of the best humans on the planet. As mental health practitioners, we spend a significant part of our day caring for the needs of young children and their families. We also spend time in consultation and support of pediatricians, teachers, mentors, and other community providers who champion children's rights. We see daily the immense undertaking that is required in caretaking, raising, teaching, healing, and inspiring.

We also believe the research around taking good care of yourself. The process of knowing and understanding yourself is directly connected to the ability to continue to show up and pour into the lives of children in healthy, productive, and sustainable ways. This chapter includes reflective journals for each of the important members of the village. The goal in completing these activities is to strengthen connections and create more ways of staying responsive and attuned to the children in your care.

These worksheets cover a diverse range of thinking and reflective styles. They include check boxes around the logistics and mechanics of the activity, self-assessment/self-reflective-based prompts, considerations for how these activities might be modified for small play groups or classrooms, and advice on connecting with other adults to teach or include them in this activity (e.g., a parent with a coparent, a parent with a grandparent, a lead teacher with a teaching assistant). In this space, we've incorporated culturally inclusive reflections that celebrate and engage these activities while honoring individual differences and developmental capacities.

Special Note: It is important to think of the worksheets and reflection pages in this chapter as a guide. The forms were created for easy and accessible use and account for different ways that individuals process and reflect. These forms were also created with effective utility in mind, taking into consideration all the different caring adults in a child's life, including those in administrative and leadership roles. Everyone takes in and processes information (particularly around feelings and emotions) differently based on their own personal identities as well as their role (i.e., parent, grandparent, nanny, teacher, school administrator, or mental health provider).

The forms have both qualitative and quantitative ratings to assess your and the child's experience with the activities in this book, and space for considering the content of activities as well as the creative and emotional process of being with your child[ren] or students. We want to make sure there is helpful and useful data, whether you are simply a parent that wants to play more with your child, a teacher planning the schedule for the day, or an educational leader thinking about different ways to engage in program development. There is also a key and legend of images provided to help support continued growth around the important areas of child development and relationship.

These forms are designed not to highlight judgment or limitation but growth in your development as a person who cares for children. We want to encourage making active steps from the concrete and logistical to the reflective or emotion-based parts of yourself. Here in this space lives the heart of attachment, relationships, and the capacity for co-regulation.

ADULT FORM A: ACTIVITY REFLECTION FORM

Name: ....   **Role in Child's Life:** ....

Number of Children: ....   **Number of Adult Helpers:** ....

Name of Activity: ....

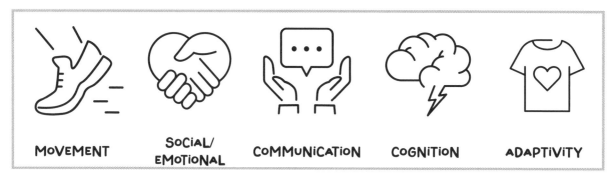

MOVEMENT   SOCIAL/EMOTIONAL   COMMUNICATION   COGNITION   ADAPTIVITY

Please circle the icons above that you believe were an area of focus during the activity with the child in your care!

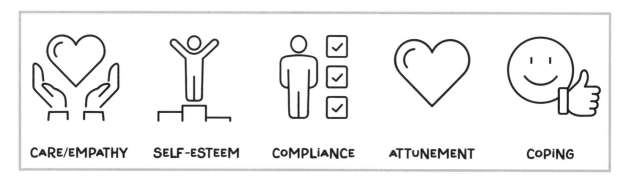

CARE/EMPATHY   SELF-ESTEEM   COMPLIANCE   ATTUNEMENT   COPING

Please circle the regulation skills that you noticed this activity aimed to address in capacity building for the child!

Reflective Ratings: In thinking about the activity you shared with the child in your care, please share your experiences with the activity, with the highest ranking (5) indicating the most enjoyable or helpful and the lowest ranking (1) being the least enjoyable or helpful:

☆ Enjoyment of the Activity (Self)   1   2   3   4   5

☆ Enjoyment of the Activity (Child)   1   2   3   4   5

☆ Logistics of Prep and Implementation of the Activity   1   2   3   4   5

☆ Level of Challenge Implementing the Activity   1   2   3   4   5

☆ Overall Experience Engaging in the Activity   1   2   3   4   5

☆ Comfort Level Teaching This Activity to Others   1   2   3   4   5

Special Note: As you shade and rank areas throughout this form, we encourage you to reflect on those data points, as they can be useful and take in more meaningful and deeper reflections about self, the children in your care, and the importance of your relationship with them.

ADULT FORM B: STRENGTHS, RESILIENCY, AND RELATIONSHIP FORM

In this reflection form, we invite and encourage you to take some time away from numbers or logistics and connect with the relational and emotional experiences you are having when participating in these activities and engaging with the child in your care. How we feel has a direct impact on how motivated we are toward engaging and interacting with others and the quality of connection we can make with them.

On this reflection page, take a closer look at various parts of your emotional experiences during the activity (activities) with your child. Take some time to think about your experience in the following ways:

Matters of the heart often involve how much care or desire we have for something. Our feelings matter a great deal and often dictate or influence when and how we make certain decisions. Our heart is also often who and what we treasure most.

The body is a very important communicator about our ability to be flexible, to mobilize, and to participate in what is happening in the world around us. Movement is important to our well-being, and it is so important for children to see our body relaxing, doing, helping, showing, and enjoying being with them.

When we are thinking, our brain is internalizing, assessing, processing, and trying to make sense of our own experiences and those of others. There are times when our environment might be overstimulating, under-stimulating, or stressful. This can impact how we might appraise a given situation.

Our energy is our enthusiasm. It is the vigor and zest for how we think, feel, and respond to our environment and what we might be doing and with whom the space is shared. Even more importantly than the words we might share, how we share and behave is motivated by our energy, and that energy is felt.

When we are in attunement with something or someone, we are calibrated, aware, focused, attentive, and present in what we are doing and whom we might be with. When we are attuned, our heart, body, brain, and energy are closely aligned in the moments or experiences we are having. Attunement does not mean perfect but present, open, and responsive.

Please take some time to shade in the circles below, based on the above descriptions. The shading should reflect and represent how much you were feeling (less shading means less engagement and more shading means higher engagement). Fill in how much your heart, body, brain, energy, and attunement were connected and engaged during the activity.

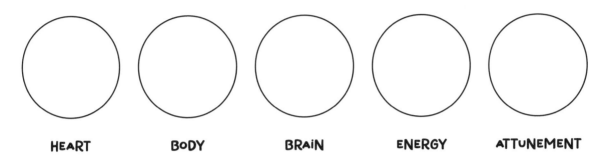

Now, take some time to view the visual representation that you just completed. Think about what you see and notice about your experience in relation to the categories above. Some circles may be shaded in more than others, some of the shading might surprise you, and others you may recognize as growth areas. All these thoughts and feelings are perfectly okay. The goal of this worksheet is to provide an opportunity that is free of judgment, to self-reflect on your own strengths and personal growth areas. This is also a space to consider and reflect on your own feelings and cultural identity while noticing how that impacts the way we show up for ourselves and the interactions with the child in our care. After taking this time for yourself, feel free to write down any meaningful reflections in the space below.

Additional notes and reflections:

ADULT FORM C: CAREGIVER/TEACHER/ PROFESSIONAL REFLECTION JOURNAL

Date: ....

Activity or Activities Reflecting On:

....

What did you and the child enjoy most about the activity, and what worked well during your time together?

....

....

....

What would you like to try differently the next time you and the child in your care engage in this activity?

....

....

....

How would you like to orient this activity to a group format within the classroom or a family inclusive activity?

....

....

....

What do you notice about yourself and your feelings and reactions during this activity?

_____

_____

_____

_____

What strengths can you identify in yourself and that of the child you are with during the activity?

_____

_____

_____

_____

What are some personal growth areas you are noticing that you would like to pay attention to when reflecting on the activity or activities with your child?

_____

_____

_____

_____

What did you learn about your child or those in your care/classroom from this activity or other activities you have tried throughout the book?

_____

_____

_____

_____

What did you learn about yourself through the eyes of the child during this activity and other activities throughout the book?

When planning, implementing, and engaging in the activities, what parts of your cultural identity showed up? What parts were happy, excited, proud, concerned, frustrated, or confused? What ways would you consider adding cultural components to the activities you implement in the future (e.g., holidays, implementing learning about individual differences, developmental capacities, use of culturally inclusive books)?

In participating in various activities throughout the book, share what you have noticed about the ways you may have been parented, taught, or cared for that have come up. Are there things you would like to adopt from those experiences? Are there other things you would like to liberate from or choose other ways of being with your child?

If so, please share more of your reflections here:

....

....

....

....

ADULT FORM D: CREATE YOUR OWN ACTIVITY TEMPLATE

Name of Activity: ....

Purpose of the Activity
Special Note(s):

....

....

Materials Needed

....

....

Instructional Guide
Step 1:

....

....

....

....

Step 2:

....

....

....

....

Step 3:

....

....

....

Step 4:

....

....

....

ANSWER KEY: DEVELOPMENT AND REGULATION SKILLS

Major Domains of Development: (1) Cognition, (2) Adaptivity, (3) Communication, (4) Motor-Physical Movement, (5) Social-Emotional Development

Regulation and Coping Goals: (A) Care, Consideration of Others, and Empathy, (B) Self-Esteem and Self-Industry, (C) Compliance and Active Listening, (D) Attunement and Being with Others, (E) Coping and Resilience

The Keepsake
Major Domains of Development: 2 ,3, 5
Regulation and Coping Goals: D, E

Today's Weather Report
Major Domains of Development: 1, 3, 5
Regulation and Coping Goals: B, E

Mirror, Mirror
Major Domains of Development: 1, 4, 5
Regulation and Coping Goals: B, D

My Sacred Space
Major Domains of Development: 2, 5
Regulation and Coping Goals: D, E

Kangaroo Comfort
Major Domains of Development: 1, 2, 3, 5
Regulation and Coping Goals: D, E

Teacher's Pet
Major Domains of Development: 1, 4, 5
Regulation and Coping Goals: A, B, C, D

The Power of Touch
Major Domains of Development: 3, 4, 5
Regulation and Coping Goals: A, D

Mindful Munching Munchkins
Major Domains of Development: 2, 3, 4, 5
Regulation and Coping Goals: C, D, E

Stop and Smell the Cookies
Major Domains of Development: 1, 3, 5
Regulation and Coping Goals: E

Resonation Station
Major Domains of Development: 2, 3, 4, 5
Regulation and Coping Goals: B, C, D

Tip of the Iceberg
Major Domains of Development: 4, 5
Regulation and Coping Goals: E

The Talking Stick
Major Domains of Development: 1, 2, 3, 4, 5
Regulation and Coping Goals: A, C, D, E

Out of the Box
Major Domains of Development: 1, 3, 4, 5
Regulation and Coping Goals: B, D, E

My Little Cookbook
Major Domains of Development: 1, 2, 3, 5
Regulation and Coping Goals: B, C

Let the Show Begin

Major Domains of Development:1, 5

Regulation and Coping Goals: B, E

Hear Me Roar

Major Domains of Development: 3, 4, 5

Regulation and Coping Goals: D, E

Mind Reader

Major Domains of Development:1, 3, 5

Regulation and Coping Goals: A, C, D

Saanvi Says

Major Domains of Development:1, 3, 4, 5

Regulation and Coping Goals: B, C, D

Once Upon a Time

Major Domains of Development:1, 3, 5

Regulation and Coping Goals: A, C, D

Feel the Rainbow

Major Domains of Development: 1, 3,4,5

Regulation and Coping Goals: B, C,D,E

CHAPTER 5

RESOURCES FOR THE VILLAGE

We hope that you have enjoyed the activities and worksheets in this book! Additionally, we understand that when it comes to caring for children, the quest for answers and guidance is continuous, and it truly does take a village to care for a child. We recognize that these activities and worksheets only help fill in a small gap to fuel the development of self-regulation skills and that sometimes more assistance and support is required. Therefore, we wanted to offer resources to continue the learning process. We wish you all the best with the children in your lives, and we hope you continue to deepen your relationship with them—they truly are the most valuable resource!

BOOKS FOR ADULTS, PROFESSIONALS, AND TEACHERS

Parenting from the Inside Out: How a Deeper Self-Understanding Can Help You Raise Children Who Thrive by Daniel Siegal, MD, and Mary Hartzell, MEd

The Whole-Brain Child: 12 Revolutionary Strategies to Nurture Your Child's Developing Mind by Daniel Siegal, MD, and Tina Payne Bryson, PhD

The Yes Brain: How to Cultivate Courage, Curiosity, and Resilience in Your Child by Daniel Siegal, MD, and Tina Payne Bryson, PhD

The Bottom Line for Baby: From Sleep Training to Screens, Thumb Sucking to Tummy Time— What the Science Says by Tina Payne Bryson, PhD

The Power of Showing Up: How Parental Presence Shapes Who Our Kids Become and How Their Brains Get Wired by Daniel Siegal, MD, and Tina Payne Bryson, PhD

No Drama Discipline: The Whole-Brain Way to Calm the Chaos and Nurture Your Child's Developing Mind by Daniel Siegal, MD, and Tina Payne Bryson, PhD

Positive Discipline: The Classic Guide to Helping Children Develop Self-Discipline, Responsibility, Cooperation, and Problem-Solving Skills by Jane Nelsen, EdD

Positive Discipline A–Z: 1001 Solutions to Everyday Parenting Problems by Jane Nelsen, EdD, Lynn Lott, MA, MFT, and H. Stephen Glenn

Positive Discipline in the Classroom: Developing Mutual Respect, Cooperation, and Responsibility in Your Classroom by Jane Nelsen, EdD, and Lynn Lott, MA, MFT, and H. Stephen Glenn

Hold On to Your Kids: Why Parents Need to Matter More Than Peers by Gordon Neufeld, PhD, and Gabor Mate, MD

Raising a Secure Child by Kent Hoffman, Glen Cooper, and Bert Powell

How to Talk So Kids Will Listen & Listen So Kids Will Talk by Adele Faber and Elaine Mazlish

BOOKS FOR CHILDREN

The Rabbit Listened by Cori Doerrfeld

The Color Monster: A Story About Emotions by Anna llenas

In My Heart: A Book of Feelings by Jo Witek

The Pout-Pout Fish by Deborah Diesen

You're My Little Cuddle Bug by Nicola Edwards

Grumpy Monkey by Suzanne Lang

My Mouth Is a Volcano by Julia Cook

Someone to Be With by Deidre Quinlan

We're Different, We're the Same by Bobbi Jane Kates

WEBSITES

American Academy of Pediatrics: www.aap.org

Healthy Children AAP Parenting: www.healthychildren.org

Child Mind Institute: www.childmind.org

Understood: www.understood.org

Parents: www.parents.com

The National Traumatic Stress Network: www.nctsn.org

CDC Children's Mental Health: www.cdc.gov/childrensmentalhealth

Collaborative for Academic, Social, and Emotional Learning (CASEL): www.casel.org

TRAiNiNGS/CERTiFiCATiONS

As professionals, it is crucial to engage in ongoing training and certifications, especially if children are the primary audience served. The trainings and certifications below are focused on providing increased knowledge and skills around attachment and relationships. Additionally, it is critical to think about children and families holistically; therefore, training and certifications should focus on increasing your professional understanding of diversity, equity, inclusion, and belonging (DEIB) to better serve children.

The Circle of Security International (Parent and Teacher Versions):
www.circleofsecurityinternational.com

Child-Parent Psychotherapy: www.childparentpsychotherapy.com

Perinatal Mental Health Certification Program:
www.postpartum.net/professionals/certification

Positive Discipline Certification (Caregiver and Teacher Versions):
www.positivediscipline.com/training

Zones of Regulation: www.zonesofregulation.com

REFERENCES

Center for Disease Control and Prevention. *Developmental Milestone Checklist for WIC (2023).* Retrieved from https://www.cdc.gov/ncbddd/wicguide/wic-developmental-milestone -checklists.html.

Fraiberg, Selma. *Clinical Studies in Infant Mental Health: The First Year of Life.* New York, NY: Basic Books, 1980.

Landreth, Garry L. *Play Therapy: The Art of the Relationship.* New York, NY: Routledge, 2012.

Lerner, Richard M., Lynn S. Liben, and Ulrich Mueller. *Handbook of Child Psychology and Developmental Science, Cognitive Processes, Vol. 2.* Hoboken, NJ: Wiley, 2015.

Parten, Mildred Bernice. "Social Participation among Preschool Children." *The Journal of Abnormal and Social Psychology,* 27 (1932): 243.

Parten, Mildred Bernice. "Social Play among Preschool Children." *The Journal of Abnormal and Social Psychology,* 28 (1933): 136–147.

Pellegrini, Anthony D., ed. *The Oxford Handbook of the Development of Play.* New York, NY: Oxford University Press, 2011.

Piaget, Jean. *The Child's Conception of the World.* London, England: Routledge & Kegan Paul, 1929.

Piaget, Jean. *The Origins of Intelligence in Children.* M. Cook, Trans. New York, NY: International University Press, 1952.

Piaget, Jean. *Play, Dreams and Imitation in Childhood*. New York, NY: W. W. Norton & Company, 1962.

Simpson, Jeffry A., W. Steven Rholes, Jami Eller, and R. L. Paetzold. "Major Principles of Attachment Theory" In *Social Psychology: Handbook of Basic Principles*. New York, NY: Guilford Press (2020): 222–239.

Skene, Kayleigh, Christine M. O'Farrelly, Elizabeth M. Byrne, Natalie Kirby, Eloise C. Stevens, and Paul G. Ramchandani. "Can Guidance during Play Enhance Children's Learning and Development in Educational Contexts? A Systematic Review and Meta-Analysis." *Child Development* 93, no. 4 (2022): 1162–1180.

Sow, Aminatou, and Ann Friedman. *Big Friendship: How We Keep Each Other Close*. New York, NY: Simon and Schuster, 2020.

Vygotsky, L. S. *Play and Its Role in the Mental Development of the Child. Soviet Psychology*, 5, 6–18, 1967.

Vygotsky, L. S. *Mind in Society: Development of Higher Psychological Processes*. Edited by Michael Cole, Vera Jolm-Steiner, Sylvia Scribner, and Ellen Souberman. Cambridge, MA: Harvard University Press, 1978. https://doi.org/10.2307/j.ctvjf9vz4.

Whitaker, Julia, and Alison Tonkin. *Play for Health Across the Lifespan: Stories from the Seven Ages of Play*. New York, NY: Routledge, 2021.

Yogman, Michael, Andrew Garner, Jeffrey Hutchinson, Kathy Hirsh-Pasek, Roberta Michnick Golinkoff, Rebecca Baum, Thresia Gambon et al. "The Power of Play: A Pediatric Role in Enhancing Development in Young Children." *Pediatrics* 142, no. 3 (2018).

Zubler, Jennifer M., Lisa D. Wiggins, Michelle M. Macias, Toni M. Whitaker, Judith S. Shaw, Jane K. Squires, Julie A. Pajek et al. "Evidence-Informed Milestones for Developmental Surveillance Tools." *Pediatrics* 149, no. 3 (2022).

ACKNOWLEDGMENTS

We want to acknowledge all the caring adults who have been present throughout our lives and as our lives continue. We want to thank all the caring adults who were pivotal in our professional and personal development. Thank you to our caregivers, extended family, teachers/professors, mentors, coaches, supervisors, and friends. You know who you are.

ABOUT THE AUTHORS

Abbré McClain is a psychologist and assistant professor at a leading institution centered around social justice and socially responsible practice, as well as the co-owner of Chicago Wellness Center for Families, PLLC. Holding strong values rooted in activism, community, and the beauty of diversity, Dr. McClain has spent over 10 years servicing youth and their families, with expertise in trauma-informed care, multicultural psychology, family wellness, and the assessment and treatment of very young children. She holds an Infant Parent Psychotherapy Endowment and certifications in Diagnostic Assessment for Young Children (DC:0-5) and Circle of Security-Parenting Facilitation (COSP) and is eligible for board certification for Perinatal Mental Health (PMH-C). Dr. McClain's understanding of wellness is positioned from a strength-based and family-centered approach. She is heavily involved in her local neighborhood community and enjoys learning about different cultures in Chicago. When not involved in outreach and care, Dr. McClain enjoys spending time with family and friends and engaging in the arts and culture in her city. She is an avid sports fan.

Jacqueline Salazar is a psychologist with over 10 years of experience serving the needs of youth in Chicagoland communities. She is passionate about fostering positive connections between families and communities they are a part of. She holds numerous certifications that specialize in trauma, addiction, and parenting approaches, such as Trauma-Focused Cognitive Behavioral Therapy (TF-CBT) and Teaching Parenting the Positive Discipline Way. Additionally, Dr. Salazar serves as part of the leadership team at a leading nonprofit institution that partners with Chicago Public Schools to help provide students with a community of support, as well as co-owns a therapy practice that specializes in therapy and consultation services for children and families. Currently, Dr. Salazar resides with her husband and son in the Southside of Chicago, where she was born and raised. She enjoys thrift shopping, horror movies, and spending quality time with family and friends.